INSTITUTION OF CIVIL ENGINEERS

MANAGEMENT DEVELOPMENT
in the construction industry

guidelines for the professional engineer

IͳI Thomas Telford, London

Management Development Working Party

C. Penny, *Chairman*, Balfour Beatty Fairclough

J. R. Deacon, Cornwall County Council

K. C. Gower, Personnel Management Consultant for Laings Civil Engineering

D. Hattersley, R. O'Rourke & Sons Ltd

C. J. White, Scott Wilson Kirkpatrick, formerly with Travers Morgan

Published for the Institution of Civil Engineers by Thomas Telford Services Ltd, Thomas Telford House, 1 Heron Quay, London E14 4JD

First published 1992
Reprinted March 1992, April 1992

ISBN 0 7277 1677 8

© The Institution of Civil Engineers, 1992

Printed in England by Staples Printers Rochester Limited

Foreword

During the 1980s a great awareness developed in the United Kingdom of the need for more purposeful management training and development both in industry and the professions. This has been highlighted by increased competition in Europe and elsewhere in the industrial world.

The Institution of Civil Engineers therefore decided to review the professional development of its membership and, in particular, management training.

Aware of the wide range of demands made on the civil engineer as a manager and that the major sectors of the industry had reviewed their needs independently, the Institution considered that a structured approach could prove beneficial to career development and be of use to individuals and organizations alike.

A working party was set up to identify

- the management training requirements for progressive stages of career development in the various sectors of the industry
- core management training needs common to these sectors of the industry
- how the Institution could best serve to help meet the management development needs of the membership.

Their report identified the different levels of management in the industry, core areas of management competency and the required levels of competence at different career stages. It also recommended that information should be presented in a format that individual members could use and which organizations could adopt or modify to suit their own staff development practices.

To test the efficiency of the recommendations, representatives of engineers at all levels of management were invited to a working seminar in June 1991. They were split into syndicates, with senior and junior managers equally distributed from the industry sectors represented - contractors, consultants, the public sector and academe.

The result is the publication of these guidelines, which will benefit individuals and organizations in the construction industry.

Contents

Preface

The progressive development of management competence has greater relevance to the professional engineer of today than ever before. Therefore to manage, the engineer must recognize the competencies that need to be developed and take responsibility for seeing that these are acquired.

Use of this document allows individuals to assess, identify and plan for the acquisition of levels of management competence at appropriate career stages. It also provides a basis on which an organization can structure a management development programme to meet its own particular needs.

It is correct to emphasize the importance of individuals taking responsibility for their development, but the need for employers to provide support is equally important. It is therefore hoped

- that employers will respond either by adopting use of this document for their organization, or ensuring that their employees are encouraged to discuss their use of it with their boss or other more senior member of staff
- that every assistance is provided to staff, consistent with the aims and objectives of the organization, to help them meet the development actions the use of this document identifies.

The Institution of Civil Engineers, through its Training Department, provides a database, which is available to individuals and organizations, geared to the development requirements likely to result from the use of this document.

1. Introduction and background

Management development needs differ from person to person depending on their particular circumstances and aspirations. It is therefore important that individuals take responsibility in the first instance for their own development.

'Management' in the construction industry has been identified in terms of ten key roles, each comprising a number of elements. The elements require different levels of competence at different career stages and model competencies have been produced that are representative across all sectors of the industry.

The key roles and the associated model competencies are central to these guidelines. They provide a diagnostic tool that invites self-assessment and comparison, allowing individuals to determine for themselves their management development needs.

It must be stressed that the model competencies are not in any way prescriptive. They serve as a means by which individuals can test their own development and identify further areas in which they could usefully apply themselves.

During the preparation of this document it became clear that there is a commonality in management development within all sectors of the industry. Further, it was accepted that the young manager today is much more likely to move across sectors for career development than was the case in the past. For this reason, sector-specific elements have been omitted from the key roles, although organizations are encouraged to introduce such additional elements to meet their specific requirements.

2. Key roles

The ten key roles of management in the construction industry and the key purpose for each are as follows.

Key role 1: Working with people
Key purpose: The skills necessary to select, motivate and lead people in order to maximize performance

Key role 2: Communications and presentations
Key purpose: Effective communication both written and verbal with business associates, clients, the media and the public

Key role 3: Professional, commercial and contractual practice
Key purpose: Development of the professional, commercial, contractual and legal factors affecting an organization

Key role 4: Project management
Key purpose: The multi-faceted responsibilities necessary to programme, monitor and control all aspects of a project from inception to successful completion

Key role 5: Information technology
Key purpose: Understanding the potential, where to obtain and how to apply information technology to best advantage

Key role 6: Marketing and publicity
Key purpose: The execution of marketing management from development of the initial strategy through to execution

Key role 7: Financial management and systems
Key purpose: The systems necessary to monitor and control all aspects of the financial well-being of an organization with a view to maximizing profit

Key role 8: Corporate management
Key purpose: Identification of corporate management objectives, development of the organizational structure and understanding of the legal criteria affecting the organization

Key role 9: Health and safety
Key purpose: Importance of an employer's responsibility and of individual accountability; establishment of safety organization, policy and training

Key role 10: Quality management

Key purpose: The need for quality; an understanding of the procedures and mechanisms for ensuring that an appropriate standard is achieved

In ordering the key roles no attempt has been made to ascribe relative priorities. Some deal with interpersonal skills which are important to managers; others deal with techniques or instruments of management. The key roles dealing with health and safety and quality could have been incorporated in other key roles, but they are considered to be so important that they have been presented separately.

The elements of each key role have been selected as both important and relevant. They have been limited to those identified as applicable to all sectors of the industry. The number of elements should not be construed as implying levels of significance. It is important to establish clear interpretations of the elements and thus they are defined for the purpose of this document in the glossary to obviate the likelihood of them meaning different things to different people.

3. Management levels

The level of competence in the elements is dependent on particular career stages, and so these need to be defined.

The career stages adopted respect job titles that have universal usage in the industry and also indicate typical levels of responsibility so that, irrespective of sector, individuals can identify their present level and their next likely level.

The job titles and responsibilities used are as follows.

Top management

Typical job titles: Chief executives, directors, partners, or most senior professional person in an organization or deputy in a large organization

Typical responsibilities: Strategic management of organizations, in addition to the general management of the business plan for the current year

Senior management

Typical job titles: Construction Manager, Associate, Divisional Director/Manager, Chief Engineer

Typical responsibilities: Management of a major sector or function of an organization; a degree of autonomy of control reporting to top management

Middle management

Typical job titles: Senior Project Engineer, Senior Project Manager, Senior Site Manager

Typical responsibilities: Management of a major project or a number of concurrent projects, including overseeing the teams working on them

Supervisory management

Typical job titles: Section Engineer, Senior Engineer, Project Engineer, Project Manager

Typical responsibilities: Management of a small project or a small team, requiring professional and financial judgement with minimum supervision

Junior management

Typical job titles: Engineer, Assistant Engineer, Graduate Engineer, Junior Engineer

Typical responsibilities: Obtaining experience at the discretion of others, normally in the early stages of their career; taking key roles in teams as individuals, exercising direction of others on a project or part of a large project

4. Levels of competence

There are four levels of competence. Each element of the key roles has the appropriate level ascribed at progressive stages of career development.

The levels of competence used are

A	Appreciation	Know what is meant by a term and what its purpose is
K	Knowledge	Understand in some detail the principles of the topic and how they are applied
E	Experience	Have acquired knowledge and skill
B	Ability	Be able to apply skill with satisfactory results

The indication of competence at varying career stages for each element in all the key roles produces the model competencies given in section 6.

The model competencies accept that competence is either being obtained, kept current or being lost. These conditions are illustrated by arrows to represent progressive acquisition of competence, the level at which competence is to be sustained and that the competence is likely to regress from the initial peak and/or previous level indicated.

5. How to use this document

Step 1. Current management level
Identify your current management level from section 3. In most cases either the job title you have will match one of those in section 3 or you will be able to match your responsibilities with those shown as typical. However, if you consider you fall between the categories listed or are not sure whether you are on one level or the next, opt for the higher level.

Step 2. Self-assessment
Self-assessment and audit forms are given at the back of this document for you to conduct your self-assessment. There is a form for each key role and you can use each form three times. These forms subsequently allow identification of your needs.

Using A, K, E or B as defined in section 4, consider your competence in each element in all the key roles. You do not have to assess against key roles or elements that you know have absolutely no relevance to you or the job you do. You need to be aware that they do have relevance to 'management' and may therefore become relevant in time.

An example of self-assessment is shown in Fig. 1.

Step 3. Comparison with model competencies
Overlay your self-assessment and audit form on the appropriate model competency in section 6 and determine whether you match, exceed or fall short of the competency given for the level at which you are assessing yourself. Record your assessment on the audit part of the self-assessment and audit forms, as shown in the

Fig. 1. Example of self-assessment

KEY ROLE 1		WORKING WITH PEOPLE															
SELF-ASSESSMENT AND AUDIT	ELEMENTS	INTERVIEW SKILLS	EMPLOYMENT CONDITIONS	INDUSTRIAL RELATIONS	STRESS MANAGEMENT	PERFORMANCE APPRAISAL	TRAINING AND DEVELOPMENT	LEADERSHIP	NEGOTIATION	DECISION MAKING	JOB EVALUATION	DELEGATION	MOTIVATION	TIME MANAGEMENT			
		1	2	3	4	5	6	7	8	9	10	11	12	13	14	15	16	17
Management level at which	B	B			B		B			B	B	B		B				
Assessment carried out :	E					E		E	E				E				
MIDDLE MANAGEMENT	K		K	K													
Date 9·6·92	A																

WORKING WITH PEOPLE

MODEL COMPETENCIES	ELEMENTS	INTERVIEW SKILLS (1)	EMPLOYMENT CONDITIONS (2)	INDUSTRIAL RELATIONS (3)	STRESS MANAGEMENT (4)	PERFORMANCE APPRAISAL (5)	TRAINING AND DEVELOPMENT (6)	LEADERSHIP (7)	NEGOTIATION (8)	DECISION MAKING (9)	JOB EVALUATION (10)	DELEGATION (11)	MOTIVATION (12)	TIME MANAGEMENT (13)	14	15	16	17
TOP MANAGEMENT - Chief Executive - Director - Partners - Senior Professional Person	B				B			B		B		B	B	B				
	E	E				E	E		E									
	K		K	K							K							
	A																	
SENIOR MANAGEMENT - Construction Manager - Associate - Divisional Director/Manager - Chief Engineer	B				B	B	B	B	B	B	B	B	B	B				
	E	E		E														
	K		K															
	A																	
MIDDLE MANAGEMENT - Senior Project Engineer - Senior Project Manager - Senior Site Manager	B				B	B	B			B		B	B	B				
	E	E	E	E				E	E		E							
	K																	
	A																	

Management level at which Assessment carried out : *MIDDLE MANAGEMENT* Date 9.6.92	B	B			B		B			B	B	B		B				
	---	---	---	---	---	---	---	---	---	---	---	---	---	---	---	---	---	---
	E					E		E	E				E					
	K		k	K														
	A																	
Assessment as model					✓		✓	✓	✓	✓		✓		✓				
Assessment greater than model		✓									✓							
Assessment less than model			✓	✓		✓							✓					
ELEMENTS FOR ACTION			*	*					*				*					
Management level at which Assessment carried out : Date	B																	
	E																	
	K																	
	A																	
Assessment as model																		
Assessment greater than model																		
Assessment less than model																		
ELEMENTS FOR ACTION																		

*Elements for action

Fig. 2. Example of audit

example in Fig. 2. By folding the forms along the dotted lines you can make direct comparison of your competence with that shown as the model and record the results.

An example of an audit is shown in Fig. 2.

Step 4. Identify priorities

From your audit identify elements that you consider require action. These may not be just those for which your assessment is less than the model competence; for example, your assessment may well match the model for a certain element which you regard as very important and therefore requiring further development. No matter how much you try to limit the number of elements you identify as requiring action, it is likely that there will be too many for you to deal with them all in a reasonable period of time. To reduce the number to something manageable you will need to adopt a procedure which allows you to identify your priorities.

The real test of priority is derived from your current responsibilities and whether or not you need the particular competence you are considering to do your job better, more efficiently or effectively, or in preparation for your next career step.

To help reach such conclusions the answers you give to the following three questions will help.

■ Is the competence relevant to your job?
■ Do you need the competence now or later?
■ How much knowledge, experience and ability do you already possess?

If you conclude you would be more effective in your job were you skilled in a particular element, that you need that skill now and that you do not have sufficient knowledge, experience or ability in the subject, it must become a priority for your action.

Alternatively you may decide that there is a matter about which your self-assessment fell short of the model and that it is something you can see would be useful. However, you conclude it has no immediate relevance in terms of your current responsibilities. In such circumstances you cannot give it priority.

Your aim is to arrive at the minimum number of priority areas for action. You will be wise to address no more than three items at a time. You can bring fresh items into consideration when you have achieved those you have already addressed.

Step 5. Taking action

Having determined areas for development you must establish an action plan that sets a timetable, addresses how you will achieve your objectives and tests the appropriateness of your decisions. This is in many ways the most important step. Section 7 provides guidance on how to develop an action plan.

If your self-assessment and audit produces few or no elements requiring action at the management level at which you made the assessment, you should repeat the process for the next career stage and identify elements for action that are of a developmental nature.

Summary

Using this document involves a five-step procedure.

- Determine current or next level of management.
- Carry out a self-assessment against the key roles.
- Compare assessment with model competencies.
- Audit results and determine priorities.
- Take action.

You can use this procedure for basic self-improvement or whenever you feel your circumstances have changed for whatever reason, i.e. you have increased responsibility, a change of employer or have achieved previous actions you set yourself.

Although this document is not intended to be in any way mandatory or prescriptive, it provides candidates for admission to membership of the Institution and reviewers with a clear insight of the order of management skills required at Professional Review. The Institution therefore encourages candidates to enclose a self-assessment, audit and action plan as part of their sumission. Candidates are expected at their Professional Review to have the competencies equal to or greater than those indicated for junior management.

6. Model competencies

CPD : ICE MANAGEMENT DEVELOPMENT

KEY ROLE 1 — WORKING WITH PEOPLE

MODEL COMPETENCIES

MANAGEMENT LEVEL	ELEMENTS	1 INTERVIEW SKILLS	2 EMPLOYMENT CONDITIONS	3 INDUSTRIAL RELATIONS	4 STRESS MANAGEMENT	5 PERFORMANCE APPRAISAL	6 TRAINING AND DEVELOPMENT	7 LEADERSHIP	8 NEGOTIATION	9 DECISION MAKING	10 JOB EVALUATION	11 DELEGATION	12 MOTIVATION	13 TIME MANAGEMENT	14	15	16	17
TOP MANAGEMENT – Chief Executive – Director – Partners – Senior Professional Person	B				B			B		B		B	B	B				
	E	E				E	E		E									
	K		K	K							K							
	A																	
SENIOR MANAGEMENT – Construction Manager – Associate – Divisional Director/Manager – Chief Engineer	B				B	B	B	B	B	B	B	B	B	B				
	E	E		E														
	K		K															
	A																	
MIDDLE MANAGEMENT – Senior Project Engineer – Senior Project Manager – Senior Site Manager	B				B	B	B			B		B	B	B				
	E	E	E	E				E	E		E							
	K																	
	A																	
SUPERVISORY MANAGEMENT – Section Engineer – Senior Engineer – Project Engineer – Project Manager	B													B				
	E					E	E	E	E		E	E	E					
	K	K	K	K					K		K							
	A																	
JUNIOR MANAGEMENT – Engineer – Graduate Engineer – Assistant Engineer – Junior Engineer	B																	
	E													E				
	K				K		K	K		K		K	K					
	A	A	A	A		A			A		A							

INITIAL PEAK COMPETENCE LEVEL

LEVELS OF COMPETENCE

- A Appreciation : Know what is meant by the term and what its purpose is.
- E Experience : Acquisition of knowledge and skill.
- K Knowledge : Understand in some detail the principles of the topic and how they are applied.
- B Ability : Application of skill with satisfactory results.

 PROGRESSIVE   SUSTAINED   REGRESSIVE

CPD : ICE MANAGEMENT DEVELOPMENT

KEY ROLE 2 — COMMUNICATIONS AND PRESENTATIONS

MODEL COMPETENCIES

MANAGEMENT LEVEL	ELEMENTS	WRITTEN COMMUNICATION	ORAL PRESENTATION	TELECOMMUNICATION	MANAGEMENT OF MEETINGS	BUSINESS PRESENTATIONS	PUBLIC MEETINGS	DEALING WITH MEDIA AND VIP'S	FOREIGN LANGUAGES	9	10	11	12	13	14	15	16	17
		1	2	3	4	5	6	7	8	9	10	11	12	13	14	15	16	17
TOP MANAGEMENT — Chief Executive, Director, Partners, Senior Professional Person	B	B	B	B	B	B	B	B										
	E								E									
	K																	
	A																	
SENIOR MANAGEMENT — Construction Manager, Associate, Divisional Director/Manager, Chief Engineer	B	B	B	B	B	B	B	B										
	E								E									
	K																	
	A																	
MIDDLE MANAGEMENT — Senior Project Engineer, Senior Project Manager, Senior Site Manager	B	B				B	B											
	E		E	E	E			E	E									
	K																	
	A																	
SUPERVISORY MANAGEMENT — Section Engineer, Senior Engineer, Project Engineer, Project Manager	B																	
	E	E	E	E	E	E	E		E									
	K							K										
	A																	
JUNIOR MANAGEMENT — Engineer, Graduate Engineer, Assistant Engineer, Junior Engineer	B													INITIAL PEAK				
	E	E		E					E					COMPETENCE				
	K		K		K	K	K							LEVEL				
	A							A										

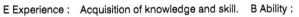

LEVELS OF COMPETENCE

A Appreciation : Know what is meant by the term and what its purpose is.

E Experience : Acquisition of knowledge and skill.

K Knowledge : Understand in some detail the principles of the topic and how they are applied.

B Ability : Application of skill with satisfactory results.

 PROGRESSIVE   SUSTAINED   ➡ REGRESSIVE

KEY ROLE 3 — PROFESSIONAL COMMERCIAL AND CONTRACTUAL PRACTICE

MODEL COMPETENCIES

MANAGEMENT LEVEL	ELEMENTS	1 PROFESSIONAL ETHICS AND RULES OF CONDUCT	2 CONTRACTUAL ARRANGEMENTS	3 CONTRACTS AND AGREEMENTS	4 COMMERCIAL NEGOTIATION	5 CLAIMS DISPUTES AND LITIGATION PROCEDURES	6 CONDITIONS OF CONTRACT	7 CONDITIONS OF ENGAGEMENTS	8 RISK MANAGEMENT INCLUDING INSURANCE	9 PROCUREMENT PROCEDURES	10	11	12	13	14	15	16	17
TOP MANAGEMENT — Chief Executive, Director, Partners, Senior Professional Person	B	B	B	B	B		B	B	B	B								
	E					E												
	K																	
	A																	
SENIOR MANAGEMENT — Construction Manager, Associate, Divisional Director/Manager, Chief Engineer	B	B	B	B	B		B											
	E					E		E	E	E								
	K																	
	A																	
MIDDLE MANAGEMENT — Senior Project Engineer, Senior Project Manager, Senior Site Manager	B																	
	E	E	E	E	E	E	E	E										
	K								K	K								
	A																	
SUPERVISORY MANAGEMENT — Section Engineer, Senior Engineer, Project Engineer, Project Manager	B																	
	E		E															
	K	K		K	K	K	K	K	K	K								
	A																	
JUNIOR MANAGEMENT — Engineer, Graduate Engineer, Assistant Engineer, Junior Engineer	B																	
	E																	
	K		K															
	A	A		A	A	A	A	A	A	A								

INITIAL PEAK COMPETENCE LEVEL

LEVELS OF COMPETENCE

A Appreciation : Know what is meant by the term and what its purpose is.

K Knowledge : Understand in some detail the principles of the topic and how they are applied.

E Experience : Acquisition of knowledge and skill.

B Ability : Application of skill with satisfactory results.

  PROGRESSIVE   SUSTAINED    REGRESSIVE

CPD : ICE MANAGEMENT DEVELOPMENT

KEY ROLE 4	PROJECT MANAGEMENT

MODEL COMPETENCIES

	ELEMENTS	PRECONTRACT ACTIVITIES	PROGRAMMING WORK	RESOURCE PLANNING	STAFFING AND RESPONSIBILITIES	SUB-CONTRACTORS	PROGRESS MONITORING AND CONTROL	FINANCIAL CONTROL	TEAM LEADERSHIP	CERTIFICATION AND PAYMENT	CLIENT RELATIONS	ENVIRONMENTAL AWARENESS						
MANAGEMENT LEVEL		1	2	3	4	5	6	7	8	9	10	11	12	13	14	15	16	17
TOP MANAGEMENT	B	B			B		B	B	B	B	B							
- Chief Executive	E		E	E		E						E						
- Director	K																	
- Partners																		
- Senior Professional Person	A																	
SENIOR MANAGEMENT	B	B	B	B	B	B	B	B	B	B	B		INITIAL PEAK					
- Construction Manager	E											E	COMPETENCE					
- Associate	K												LEVEL					
- Divisional Director/Manager																		
- Chief Engineer	A																	
MIDDLE MANAGEMENT	B																	
- Senior Project Engineer	E	E	E	E	E	E	E	E	E	E	E							
- Senior Project Manager	K											K						
- Senior Site Manager	A																	
SUPERVISORY MANAGEMENT	B																	
- Section Engineer	E				E	E					E							
- Senior Engineer	K	K	K	K	K		K	K	K		K	K						
- Project Engineer																		
- Project Manager	A																	
JUNIOR MANAGEMENT	B																	
- Engineer	E																	
- Graduate Engineer	K		K		K	K	K				K	K						
- Assistant Engineer																		
- Junior Engineer	A	A		A					A	A								

LEVELS OF COMPETENCE

A Appreciation : Know what is meant by the term and what its purpose is.

E Experience : Acquisition of knowledge and skill.

K Knowledge : Understand in some detail the principles of the topic and how they are applied.

B Ability : Application of skill with satisfactory results.

 PROGRESSIVE   SUSTAINED   REGRESSIVE

KEY ROLE 5 — INFORMATION TECHNOLOGY

MODEL COMPETENCIES

MANAGEMENT LEVEL	ELEMENTS	1 PRESENT STATUS & EXPECTED DEVELOPMENTS	2 COMPUTER AS A MANAGEMENT TOOL	3 IN-HOUSE COMPUTING APPLICATIONS	4 EXTERNAL COMPUTING SERVICES	5 PERSONAL COMPUTING SKILLS	6 SPECIALIST SOFTWARE	7	8	9	10	11	12	13	14	15	16	17
TOP MANAGEMENT	B																	
- Chief Executive	E		E															
- Director / - Partners	K	K		K	K	K	K											
- Senior Professional Person	A																	
SENIOR MANAGEMENT	B																	
- Construction Manager	E		E															
- Associate / - Divisional Director/Manager	K	K		K	K	K	K											
- Chief Engineer	A																	
MIDDLE MANAGEMENT	B																	
- Senior Project Engineer	E		E	E		E	E											
- Senior Project Manager	K	K			K													
- Senior Site Manager	A																	
SUPERVISORY MANAGEMENT	B																	
- Section Engineer	E			E		E	E											
- Senior Engineer / - Project Engineer	K	K	K		K													
- Project Manager	A																	
JUNIOR MANAGEMENT	B										INITIAL PEAK							
- Engineer	E					E	E				COMPETENCE LEVEL							
- Graduate Engineer / - Assistant Engineer	K		K	K	K													
- Junior Engineer	A	A																

LEVELS OF COMPETENCE

A Appreciation : Know what is meant by the term and what its purpose is.

E Experience : Acquisition of knowledge and skill.

K Knowledge : Understand in some detail the principles of the topic and how they are applied.

B Ability : Application of skill with satisfactory results.

 PROGRESSIVE   SUSTAINED   REGRESSIVE

KEY ROLE 6	MARKETING AND PUBLICITY

MODEL COMPETENCIES

	ELEMENTS	STRATEGY AND PLANNING	MARKET RESEARCH	PROMOTIONAL TECHNIQUES	PROPOSALS AND PRESENTATIONS	PUBLIC RELATIONS											
MANAGEMENT LEVEL		1	2	3	4	5	6	7	8	9	10	11	12	13	14	15	16	17
TOP MANAGEMENT	B	B			B	B				INITIAL PEAK								
- Chief Executive	E		E	E						COMPETENCE LEVEL								
- Director	K																	
- Partners	A																	
- Senior Professional Person																		
SENIOR MANAGEMENT	B																	
- Construction Manager	E	E		E	E	E												
- Associate	K		K															
- Divisional Director/Manager	A																	
- Chief Engineer																		
MIDDLE MANAGEMENT	B																	
- Senior Project Engineer	E				E	E												
- Senior Project Manager	K	K	K	K														
- Senior Site Manager	A																	
SUPERVISORY MANAGEMENT	B																	
- Section Engineer	E																	
- Senior Engineer	K	K		K	K	K												
- Project Engineer	A		A															
- Project Manager																		
JUNIOR MANAGEMENT	B																	
- Engineer	E																	
- Graduate Engineer	K																	
- Assistant Engineer	A	A		A	A	A												
- Junior Engineer																		

LEVELS OF COMPETENCE

A Appreciation : Know what is meant by the term and what its purpose is.

E Experience : Acquisition of knowledge and skill.

K Knowledge : Understand in some detail the principles of the topic and how they are applied.

B Ability : Application of skill with satisfactory results.

 PROGRESSIVE 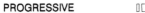 SUSTAINED   REGRESSIVE

KEY ROLE 7 — FINANCIAL MANAGEMENT AND SYSTEMS

MODEL COMPETENCIES

MANAGEMENT LEVEL	ELEMENTS	1 REPORTING SYSTEMS	2 ESTABLISHING A BUDGET	3 COST CONTROL SYSTEMS	4 CASH FLOW	5 PROFIT AND LOSS ACCOUNT	6 BALANCE SHEETS	7 VAT AND TAXATION	8 PROJECT FINANCE	9 EEC AND GOVERNMENT GRANTS	10	11	12	13	14	15	16	17
TOP MANAGEMENT — Chief Executive, Director, Partners, Senior Professional Person	B	B	B	B	B	B	B		B									
	E									E								
	K							K										
	A																	
SENIOR MANAGEMENT — Construction Manager, Associate, Divisional Director/Manager, Chief Engineer	B	B	B	B														
	E				E	E	E		E									
	K							K		K								
	A																	
MIDDLE MANAGEMENT — Senior Project Engineer, Senior Project Manager, Senior Site Manager	B																	
	E	E	E	E	E			E	E									
	K				K	K	K			K								
	A																		
SUPERVISORY MANAGEMENT — Section Engineer, Senior Engineer, Project Engineer, Project Manager	B																	
	E	E		E														
	K		K		K	K			K									
	A						A	A		A								
JUNIOR MANAGEMENT — Engineer, Graduate Engineer, Assistant Engineer, Junior Engineer	B																	
	E																	
	K	K		K														
	A		A		A	A			A									

INITIAL PEAK COMPETENCE LEVEL

LEVELS OF COMPETENCE

A Appreciation : Know what is meant by the term and what its purpose is.

E Experience : Acquisition of knowledge and skill.

K Knowledge : Understand in some detail the principles of the topic and how they are applied.

B Ability : Application of skill with satisfactory results.

 PROGRESSIVE
 SUSTAINED
 REGRESSIVE

CPD : ICE MANAGEMENT DEVELOPMENT

KEY ROLE 8 — CORPORATE MANAGEMENT

MODEL COMPETENCIES

MANAGEMENT LEVEL	ELEMENTS	1 OBJECTIVES AND CORPORATE STRATEGY	2 BUSINESS PLANS	3 ORGANIZATION AND STRUCTURE	4 ROLE OF OFFICERS	5 MEMORANDUM AND ARTICLES	6 MERGERS AND AQUISITIONS	7 FINANCIAL ARRANGEMENTS	8	9	10	11	12	13	14	15	16	17
TOP MANAGEMENT	B	B	B	B	B	B												
- Chief Executive	E						E	E				INITIAL PEAK						
- Director																		
- Partners	K											COMPETENCE LEVEL						
- Senior Professional Person	A																	
SENIOR MANAGEMENT	B																	
- Construction Manager	E	E	E	E	E													
- Associate																		
- Divisional Director/Manager	K					K	K	K										
- Chief Engineer	A																	
MIDDLE MANAGEMENT	B																	
- Senior Project Engineer	E			E														
- Senior Project Manager	K	K	K		K													
- Senior Site Manager	A					A	A	A										
SUPERVISORY MANAGEMENT	B																	
- Section Engineer	E																	
- Senior Engineer	K	K	K	K	K													
- Project Engineer	A																	
- Project Manager																		
JUNIOR MANAGEMENT	B																	
- Engineer	E																	
- Graduate Engineer	K																	
- Assistant Engineer	A	A	A	A	A													
- Junior Engineer																		

LEVELS OF COMPETENCE

A Appreciation : Know what is meant by the term and what its purpose is.

E Experience : Acquisition of knowledge and skill.

K Knowledge : Understand in some detail the principles of the topic and how they are applied.

B Ability : Application of skill with satisfactory results.

 PROGRESSIVE
 SUSTAINED
  REGRESSIVE

KEY ROLE 9 — HEALTH AND SAFETY

MODEL COMPETENCIES

MANAGEMENT LEVEL	ELEMENTS	HEALTH AND SAFETY LEGISLATION (1)	HEALTH AND SAFETY AT WORK (2)	SAFETY POLICY AND PROCEDURES (3)	SAFETY MANAGEMENT AND EDUCATION (4)	5	6	7	8	9	10	11	12	13	14	15	16	17
TOP MANAGEMENT — Chief Executive, Director, Partners, Senior Professional Person	B			B	B													
	E	E	E															
	K																	
	A								INITIAL PEAK									
SENIOR MANAGEMENT — Construction Manager, Associate, Divisional Director/Manager, Chief Engineer	B		B	B	B				COMPETENCE LEVEL									
	E	E																
	K																	
	A																	
MIDDLE MANAGEMENT — Senior Project Engineer, Senior Project Manager, Senior Site Manager	B		B															
	E	E		E	E													
	K																	
	A																	
SUPERVISORY MANAGEMENT — Section Engineer, Senior Engineer, Project Engineer, Project Manager	B																	
	E	E	E	E	E													
	K																	
	A																	
JUNIOR MANAGEMENT — Engineer, Graduate Engineer, Assistant Engineer, Junior Engineer	B																	
	E		E															
	K	K		K	K													
	A																	

LEVELS OF COMPETENCE

A Appreciation : Know what is meant by the term and what its purpose is.

E Experience : Acquisition of knowledge and skill.

K Knowledge : Understand in some detail the principles of the topic and how they are applied.

B Ability : Application of skill with satisfactory results.

  PROGRESSIVE   SUSTAINED   REGRESSIVE

KEY ROLE 10	QUALITY MANAGEMENT

MODEL COMPETENCIES

MANAGEMENT LEVEL	ELEMENTS	QUALITY POLICY AND SYSTEMS	COMPANY MANUALS AND PROCEDURES	QUALITY IMPLEMENTATION	4	5	6	7	8	9	10	11	12	13	14	15	16	17
		1	2	3	4	5	6	7	8	9	10	11	12	13	14	15	16	17
TOP MANAGEMENT	B	B																
- Chief Executive	E		E	E														
- Director	K																	
- Partners																		
- Senior Professional Person	A																	
SENIOR MANAGEMENT	B	B																
- Construction Manager	E		E	E														
- Associate	K																	
- Divisional Director/Manager																		
- Chief Engineer	A																	
MIDDLE MANAGEMENT	B		B															
- Senior Project Engineer	E	E		E														
- Senior Project Manager	K																	
- Senior Site Manager																		
	A																	
SUPERVISORY MANAGEMENT	B										INITIAL PEAK							
- Section Engineer	E	E	E	E							COMPETENCE LEVEL							
- Senior Engineer	K																	
- Project Engineer																		
- Project Manager	A																	
JUNIOR MANAGEMENT	B																	
- Engineer	E		E															
- Graduate Engineer																		
- Assistant Engineer	K	K		K														
- Junior Engineer	A																	

LEVELS OF COMPETENCE

A Appreciation : Know what is meant by the term and what its purpose is.

E Experience : Acquisition of knowledge and skill.

K Knowledge : Understand in some detail the principles of the topic and how they are applied.

B Ability : Application of skill with satisfactory results.

 PROGRESSIVE   SUSTAINED  REGRESSIVE

7. Action plan

To take full advantage of the procedure described in section 5, you must determine a course of action for your further development.

Flow chart
As shown in the flow chart in Fig. 3, your first need is to share the conclusions you reached by self-assessment with someone else.

Discussion
If you are employed you can talk them over with your boss, other colleagues, your training department or someone else whose opinion you value. If you have an appraisal procedure this would be an excellent occasion to seek confirmation that your employer agrees with how you see your development.

Disagreement
In discussion the priorities you determined might not be agreed, because other elements may be identified as more important or

Fig. 3. An action plan

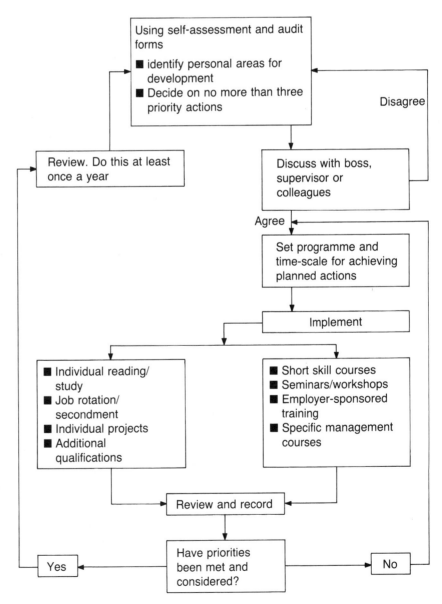

you may not be seen as being as competent as you thought. In these circumstances it is necessary to reconsider your self-assessment to see if you should reorder your priorities.

Agreement, programme and time-scale

If your discussions lead to a degree of agreement, you should establish a time-scale for achieving results. This is not only a good discipline to ensure that you will review progress but also by sharing your intentions with someone such as your boss, you give the process importance and possibly establish access to any help you may require to meet your objectives.

Implementation

The next requirement is to determine how you will achieve your planned development. This depends on your circumstances, the provisions made by your employer and, more important, on your own motivation. Typical examples of ways you may proceed are given in Fig. 3.

Routine review and recording

As you progress you must get into the habit of reviewing and recording your achievements. ICE 108 can be used as a career planner or a record of continuing professional development to remind you of your targetted development and how and when this is met.

Meeting priorities

If you can conclude, when you carry out a review on the dates you scheduled, that you have accomplished one or all of your objectives, repeat the process to establish new priorities. Should you decide you need more time then re-establish new dates on which you will review progress.

Annual overview

Irrespective of whether or not you have carried out interim reviews, you should at least once a year assess yourself to see how you are progressing and reflect on what you need to achieve in the forthcoming year.

Summary

The flow chart in Fig. 3 sets down a procedure which, if followed, will help you to develop an action plan for your continuing professional development. The process addresses some essential considerations

- that a plan for 12 months is considered, it is on a rolling basis and should cover a three-year horizon
- that wherever possible, self-assessed needs and the resulting action plan are confirmed by a totally honest appraisal with a superior or more senior person at work or a colleague whose opinions are respected

- that some form of record and subsequent assessment of achievements is kept; ICE 108 suits this purpose
- that there are a number of ways in which personal development can be achieved: it does not rely wholly on attending formal training courses
- that an action plan is an essential part of management development for professionals, whether it is after four or forty years of a career.

Glossary of terms used in the elements

Key role 1: Working with people

1. *Interview skills:* Questioning and listening techniques to acquire information in order to assess capabilities and use information obtained as appropriate.

2. *Employment conditions:* Statutory or other rules under which people are employed.

3. *Industrial relations:* A framework established to avoid conflict, which reflects the fact that employees react to their work in varying ways.

4. *Stress management:* Recognizing the consequences of pressure applied to achieve results and exercising awareness, concern and control on behalf of self and others.

5. *Performance appraisal:* A procedure by which the growth and development of individuals and organizations can be monitored and communicated to mutual advantage.

6. *Training and development:* A structured approach towards enhancing the effectiveness of people in their current work, which provides for the future needs of the individuals and the organization.

7. *Leadership:* The initiative and vision that encourages others to carry out tasks under direction.

8. *Negotiation:* Planned discussion and bargaining that consistently allows acceptable agreement to be reached.

9. *Decision-making:* Judgement exercised with responsibility once all relevant factors have been taken into account.

10. *Job evaluation:* The determination of skills required to carry out specific tasks or functions.

11. *Delegation:* The act of giving responsibility and authority for a function or task to another while remaining accountable.

12. *Motivation:* Selection of the appropriate technique with which to generate enthusiasm in self and others to produce the best performance in their duties.

13. *Time management:* The establishment of priorities that ensures objectives are met, fully recognizing time as a resource.

Key role 2: Communications and presentations

1. *Written communication:* The use of memos, letters and reports to express ideas clearly and precisely.

2. *Oral presentation:* The techniques by which ideas are communicated verbally to groups and individuals.

3. *Telecommunication:* The range of support systems available to facilitate the expression of ideas, verbally and non-verbally, from which selections are made to meet business objectives.

4. *Management of meetings:* The rules and procedures which ensure that time in meetings is planned, that all the participants contribute, that the purpose is achieved and is subsequently reported.

5. *Business presentations:* The communication of business objectives in a professional manner that recognizes the interests of clients.

6. *Public meetings:* Events arranged to enable issues of concern to a wide audience to be debated and at which the specialist input of professionals is communicated.

7. *Dealing with media and VIPs:* The skills with which a professional acts as a spokesperson, giving information that is factual in a courteous way, while remaining conscious of the implications of what is said and written.

8. *Foreign languages:* The means by which communication between the multi-cultural business markets is professionally carried out.

Key role 3: Professional, commercial and contractual practice

1. *Professional ethics and rules of conduct:* Moral, legal and professional rules under which business is conducted.

2. *Contractual arrangements:* The systems and procedures under which contracts are administered in practice.

3. *Contracts and agreements:* The general principles of law, and in particular contract law, that govern the pursuit and performance of business.

4. *Commercial negotiation:* The application of planned discussions and bargaining on behalf of an organization, clients or others, to achieve the maximum advantage.

5. *Claims, disputes and litigation procedures:* Provisions for resolving commercial disputes, as defined by the form of contract and statute.

6. *Conditions of contract:* The terms under which skills, goods or services are provided and paid for, often covered by standard forms of contract published by professional bodies or trade associations.

7. *Conditions of engagements:* The terms under which professional expertise is employed.

8. *Risk management including insurance:* The evaluation of and provisions made which reflect the areas of uncertainty in decisions taken.

9. *Procurement procedures:* The practices by which goods and services are acquired.

Key role 4: Project management

1. *Precontract activities:* The determination of requirements under the contract, the establishment of communication routes, procedures to be adopted and overall organization to be employed to meet the objectives.

2. *Programming work:* Scheduling of activities such that the agreed date for completion can be achieved.

3. *Resource planning:* Identification of the skills, goods and services needed to meet the requirements of a contract to ensure their availability as required by the programme.

4. *Staffing and responsibilities:* The identification of those able and available to perform the appropriate tasks and functions required and briefing them in respect of their duties and accountability.

5. *Subcontractors:* The identification, appointment and control of others (organizations and/or individuals) employed to meet the obligations of a contract.

6. *Progress monitoring and control:* The periodic assessment of actual performance against programmed performance allowing for corrective measures if needed.

7. *Financial control:* The establishment and monitoring of systems that enable the actual costs of the contract to be routinely determined and compared with those budgeted.

8. *Team leadership:* Accountability exercised through appropriate delegation and motivation of others carrying out tasks under direction to achieve given or set objectives.

9. *Certification and payment:* The procedures under which work done or services rendered is valued and remunerated.

10. *Client relations:* The establishment and maintenance of professional communications, on a regular or as required basis, to the employer under a contract.

11. *Environmental awareness:* Recognition of and action to limit the potential impact of planned activities on the individual, the public and society in general, and to minimize pollution and damage.

Key role 5: Information technology

1. *Present status and expected developments:* Recognition of and action to ensure that the advantages that can derive from current technology are known and hence can be used to improve business performance.

2. *The computer as a management tool:* The application of systems to provide data on which decisions can be taken.

3. *In-house computing applications:* The determination, use, development and control of data- processing to allow for improved efficiency and/or quality of services provided.

4. *External computing services:* Recognition of and use of expertise in specialist bureaux to meet needs not available in-house.

5. *Personal computing skills:* Inputting to and retrieving of information from available systems.

6. *Specialist software:* Recognition of the availability, range of product and applications met by package designers in the computing market.

Key role 6: Marketing and publicity

1. *Strategy and planning:* The general direction and means of achieving, business and organizational objectives appropriate to short/medium/long-term goals.

2. *Market research:* The systematic identification of the available opportunities, the strengths and weaknesses of competitors and the extent of future business potential.

3. *Promotional techniques:* The ways in which an organization establishes or maintains its corporate identity to attact new and repeat business from clients, e.g. advertising, visits, seminars, functions, sponsorship.

4. *Proposals and presentations:* The written or verbal techniques used to secure a business opportunity by invitation or as a consequence of targeted marketing activities.

5. *Public relations:* Those activities aimed at creating heightened corporate or product awareness, or those exercised in protection/maintenance of an established image.

Key role 7: Financial management and systems

1. *Reporting systems:* Procedures established to ensure that the day to day management of the affairs of an organization are under overall control and that information is available on which further actions can be taken as necessary.

2. *Establishing a budget:* The forecasting of expenditure and income against which controls are developed.

3. *Cost control systems:* Means by which expenditure is identified, accounted, slowed or accelerated to maximum advantage and to maintain the liquidity of an organization.

4. *Cash flow:* A measure of the cash available to the business.

5. *Profit and loss account:* A retrospective summary of the actual expenditure/income position relative to the budget position for a financial period.

6. *Balance sheet:* A statement produced at a given time showing the assets and liabilities of the business.

7. *VAT and taxation:* Government-dictated deductions from the profits of an organization, both direct and indirect.

8. *Project finance:* The methods by which clients are able to pay for the work they commission and the effects these have on the release of cash in payment for services, goods or work completed.

9. *EEC and government grants:* The availability of sources of help and incentives, for funding and acquisition of work, nationally and in the European Community.

Key role 8: Corporate management

1. *Objectives and corporate strategy:* The overall goals of an organization in terms of its product, service, capability and markets, expressed as a series of targets that translate into activities and tasks.

2. *Business plans:* A written statement of the objectives of an organization in pursuit of its goals that reflects and reports on past performance, looks forward for the next one, three and five years, examines the market and establishes financial targets used to monitor progress.

3. *Organization and structure:* The internal arrangement of a business that reflects the corporate culture and provides the support necessary for the achievement of strategic goals.

4. *Role of officers:* Appointments and responsibilities of those staff in organizations who are charged with liability in law.

5. *Memorandum and articles:* A statement required by law for all organizations seeking to limit their liability and register under the Companies Act that sets down how the requirements are to be met.

6. *Mergers and acquisitions:* Options available to organizations seeking to grow other than organically.

7. *Financial arrangements:* Means by which organizations are able to underwrite their borrowing requirements and distribute their assets to achieve their business plans.

Key role 9: Health and safety

1. *Health and safety legislation:* Recognition of the applicability of existing and pending health and safety law, the liability of all employers and the responsibilities of individuals.

2. *Health and safety at work:* Recognition of the health and safety law as applied to places of work, the liability of employers and the responsibilities of individuals.

3. *Safety policy and procedures:* The statutory requirement of employers to state their safety policy and the procedures that ensure it is carried out.

4. *Safety management and education:* The provision of routine inspections to confirm compliance with policy, that new staff are adequately inducted, that existing staff are reminded of safe working practices and that safety is addressed in all works carried out.

Key role 10: Quality management

1. *Quality policy and systems:* Recognition of the need for quality to be consciously addressed and set down as a corporate policy statement, supported by systems appropriate to the achievement of the policy.

2. *Company manuals and procedures:* Derived as appropriate from the corporate policy statement, establishing the systems, responsibilities and controls that apply.

3. *Quality implementation:* The methods by which the systems are used and the audit techniques to be used to ensure that compliance is maintained.

Self-assessment and audit

KEY ROLE 1		WORKING WITH PEOPLE

SELF-ASSESSMENT AND AUDIT

	ELEMENTS	INTERVIEW SKILLS	EMPLOYMENT CONDITIONS	INDUSTRIAL RELATIONS	STRESS MANAGEMENT	PERFORMANCE APPRAISAL	TRAINING AND DEVELOPMENT	LEADERSHIP	NEGOTIATION	DECISION-MAKING	JOB EVALUATION	DELEGATION	MOTIVATION	TIME MANAGEMENT				
		1	2	3	4	5	6	7	8	9	10	11	12	13	14	15	16	17
Management level at which	B																	
Assessment carried out :	E																	
	K																	
Date	A																	
Assessment as model																		
Assessment greater than model																		
Assessment less than model																		
ELEMENTS FOR ACTION																		
Management level at which	B																	
Assessment carried out :	E																	
	K																	
Date	A																	
Assessment as model																		
Assessment greater than model																		
Assessment less than model																		
ELEMENTS FOR ACTION																		
Management level at which	B																	
Assessment carried out :	E																	
	K																	
Date	A																	
Assessment as model																		
Assessment greater than model																		
Assessment less than model																		
ELEMENTS FOR ACTION																		

LEVELS OF COMPETENCE

A Appreciation : Know what is meant by the term and what its purpose is.

K Knowledge : Understand in some detail the principles of the topic and how they are applied.

E Experience : Acquisition of knowledge and skill.

B Ability : Application of skill with satisfactory results.

Fold along dotted lines when comparing self-assessment with model competencies

KEY ROLE 2	COMMUNICATIONS AND PRESENTATIONS

SELF-ASSESSMENT AND AUDIT

	ELEMENTS	WRITTEN COMMUNICATION	ORAL PRESENTATION	TELECOMMUNICATION	MANAGEMENT OF MEETINGS	BUSINESS PRESENTATIONS	PUBLIC MEETINGS	DEALING WITH MEDIA AND VIPs	FOREIGN LANGUAGES									
		1	2	3	4	5	6	7	8	9	10	11	12	13	14	15	16	17
Management level at which	B																	
Assessment carried out :	E																	
	K																	
Date	A																	
Assessment as model																		
Assessment greater than model																		
Assessment less than model																		
ELEMENTS FOR ACTION																		
Management level at which	B																	
Assessment carried out :	E																	
	K																	
Date	A																	
Assessment as model																		
Assessment greater than model																		
Assessment less than model																		
ELEMENTS FOR ACTION																		
Management level at which	B																	
Assessment carried out :	E																	
	K																	
Date	A																	
Assessment as model																		
Assessment greater than model																		
Assessment less than model																		
ELEMENTS FOR ACTION																		

LEVELS OF COMPETENCE

A Appreciation : Know what is meant by the term and what its purpose is.

K Knowledge : Understand in some detail the principles of the topic and how they are applied.

E Experience : Acquisition of knowledge and skill.

B Ability : Application of skill with satisfactory results.

Fold along dotted lines when comparing self-assessment with model competencies

KEY ROLE 3 — PROFESSIONAL COMMERCIAL AND CONTRACTUAL PRACTICE

SELF-ASSESSMENT AND AUDIT

	ELEMENTS	PROFESSIONAL ETHICS AND RULES OF CONDUCT	CONTRACTUAL ARRANGEMENTS	CONTRACTS AND AGREEMENTS	COMMERCIAL NEGOTIATION	CLAIMS, DISPUTES AND LITIGATION PROCEDURES	CONDITIONS OF CONTRACT	CONDITIONS OF ENGAGEMENTS	RISK MANAGEMENT INCLUDING INSURANCE	PROCUREMENT PROCEDURES								
		1	2	3	4	5	6	7	8	9	10	11	12	13	14	15	16	17
Management level at which	B																	
Assessment carried out :	E																	
	K																	
Date	A																	
Assessment as model																		
Assessment greater than model																		
Assessment less than model																		
ELEMENTS FOR ACTION																		
Management level at which	B																	
Assessment carried out :	E																	
	K																	
Date	A																	
Assessment as model																		
Assessment greater than model																		
Assessment less than model																		
ELEMENTS FOR ACTION																		
Management level at which	B																	
Assessment carried out :	E																	
	K																	
Date	A																	
Assessment as model																		
Assessment greater than model																		
Assessment less than model																		
ELEMENTS FOR ACTION																		

LEVELS OF COMPETENCE

A Appreciation : Know what is meant by the term and what its purpose is.

K Knowledge : Understand in some detail the principles of the topic and how they are applied.

E Experience : Acquisition of knowledge and skill.

B Ability : Application of skill with satisfactory results.

Fold along dotted lines when comparing self-assessment with model competencies

CPD : ICE MANAGEMENT DEVELOPMENT

KEY ROLE 4 — PROJECT MANAGEMENT

SELF-ASSESSMENT AND AUDIT

	ELEMENTS	PRECONTRACT ACTIVITIES	PROGRAMMING WORK	RESOURCE PLANNING	STAFFING AND RESPONSIBILITIES	SUBCONTRACTORS	PROGRESS MONITORING AND CONTROL	FINANCIAL CONTROL	TEAM LEADERSHIP	CERTIFICATION AND PAYMENT	CLIENT RELATIONS	ENVIRONMENTAL AWARENESS	12	13	14	15	16	17
		1	2	3	4	5	6	7	8	9	10	11	12	13	14	15	16	17
Management level at which	B																	
Assessment carried out :	E																	
	K																	
Date	A																	
Assessment as model																		
Assessment greater than model																		
Assessment less than model																		
ELEMENTS FOR ACTION																		
Management level at which	B																	
Assessment carried out :	E																	
	K																	
Date	A																	
Assessment as model																		
Assessment greater than model																		
Assessment less than model																		
ELEMENTS FOR ACTION																		
Management level at which	B																	
Assessment carried out :	E																	
	K																	
Date	A																	
Assessment as model																		
Assessment greater than model																		
Assessment less than model																		
ELEMENTS FOR ACTION																		

LEVELS OF COMPETENCE

A Appreciation : Know what is meant by the term and what its purpose is.

K Knowledge : Understand in some detail the principles of the topic and how they are applied.

E Experience : Acquisition of knowledge and skill.

B Ability : Application of skill with satisfactory results.

Fold along dotted lines when comparing self-assessment with model competencies

| KEY ROLE 5 | INFORMATION TECHNOLOGY |

SELF-ASSESSMENT AND AUDIT

	ELEMENTS	PRESENT STATUS AND EXPECTED DEVELOPMENTS	COMPUTER AS A MANAGEMENT TOOL	IN-HOUSE COMPUTING APPLICATIONS	EXTERNAL COMPUTING SERVICES	PERSONAL COMPUTING SKILLS	SPECIALIST SOFTWARE										
		1	2	3	4	5	6	7	8	9	10	11	12	13	14	15	16	17
Management level at which	B																
Assessment carried out :	E																
	K																
Date	A																
Assessment as model																	
Assessment greater than model																	
Assessment less than model																	
ELEMENTS FOR ACTION																	
Management level at which	B																
Assessment carried out :	E																
	K																
Date	A																
Assessment as model																	
Assessment greater than model																	
Assessment less than model																	
ELEMENTS FOR ACTION																	
Management level at which	B																
Assessment carried out :	E																
	K																
Date	A																
Assessment as model																	
Assessment greater than model																	
Assessment less than model																	
ELEMENTS FOR ACTION																	

LEVELS OF COMPETENCE

A Appreciation : Know what is meant by the term and what its purpose is.

K Knowledge : Understand in some detail the principles of the topic and how they are applied.

E Experience : Acquisition of knowledge and skill.

B Ability : Application of skill with satisfactory results.

Fold along dotted lines when comparing self-assessment with model competencies

KEY ROLE 6 MARKETING AND PUBLICITY

SELF-ASSESSMENT AND AUDIT	ELEMENTS	STRATEGY AND PLANNING	MARKET RESEARCH	PROMOTIONAL TECHNIQUES	PROPOSALS AND PRESENTATIONS	PUBLIC RELATIONS												
		1	2	3	4	5	6	7	8	9	10	11	12	13	14	15	16	17
Management level at which	B																	
Assessment carried out :	E																	
	K																	
Date	A																	
Assessment as model																		
Assessment greater than model																		
Assessment less than model																		
ELEMENTS FOR ACTION																		
Management level at which	B																	
Assessment carried out :	E																	
	K																	
Date	A																	
Assessment as model																		
Assessment greater than model																		
Assessment less than model																		
ELEMENTS FOR ACTION																		
Management level at which	B																	
Assessment carried out :	E																	
	K																	
Date	A																	
Assessment as model																		
Assessment greater than model																		
Assessment less than model																		
ELEMENTS FOR ACTION																		

LEVELS OF COMPETENCE

A Appreciation : Know what is meant by the term and what its purpose is.

K Knowledge : Understand in some detail the principles of the topic and how they are applied.

E Experience : Acquisition of knowledge and skill.

B Ability : Application of skill with satisfactory results.

Fold along dotted lines when comparing self-assessment with model competencies

KEY ROLE 7		FINANCIAL MANAGEMENT AND SYSTEMS																

SELF-ASSESSMENT AND AUDIT

	ELEMENTS	REPORTING SYSTEMS	ESTABLISHING A BUDGET	COST CONTROL SYSTEMS	CASH FLOW	PROFIT AND LOSS ACCOUNT	BALANCE SHEET	VAT AND TAXATION	PROJECT FINANCE	EEC AND GOVERNMENT GRANTS								
		1	2	3	4	5	6	7	8	9	10	11	12	13	14	15	16	17
Management level at which	B																	
Assessment carried out :	E																	
	K																	
Date	A																	
Assessment as model																		
Assessment greater than model																		
Assessment less than model																		
ELEMENTS FOR ACTION																		
Management level at which	B																	
Assessment carried out :	E																	
	K																	
Date	A																	
Assessment as model																		
Assessment greater than model																		
Assessment less than model																		
ELEMENTS FOR ACTION																		
Management level at which	B																	
Assessment carried out :	E																	
	K																	
Date	A																	
Assessment as model																		
Assessment greater than model																		
Assessment less than model																		
ELEMENTS FOR ACTION																		

LEVELS OF COMPETENCE

A Appreciation : Know what is meant by the term and what its purpose is.

K Knowledge : Understand in some detail the principles of the topic and how they are applied.

E Experience : Acquisition of knowledge and skill.

B Ability : Application of skill with satisfactory results.

Fold along dotted lines when comparing self-assessment with model competencies

KEY ROLE 8 — CORPORATE MANAGEMENT

SELF-ASSESSMENT AND AUDIT	ELEMENTS	OBJECTIVES AND CORPORATE STRATEGY	BUSINESS PLANS	ORGANIZATION AND STRUCTURE	ROLE OF OFFICERS	MEMORANDUM AND ARTICLES	MERGERS AND AQUISITIONS	FINANCIAL ARRANGEMENTS									
		1	2	3	4	5	6	7	8	9	10	11	12	13	14	15	16	17
Management level at which	B																	
Assessment carried out :	E																	
	K																	
Date	A																	
Assessment as model																		
Assessment greater than model																		
Assessment less than model																		
ELEMENTS FOR ACTION																		
Management level at which	B																	
Assessment carried out :	E																	
	K																	
Date	A																	
Assessment as model																		
Assessment greater than model																		
Assessment less than model																		
ELEMENTS FOR ACTION																		
Management level at which	B																	
Assessment carried out :	E																	
	K																	
Date	A																	
Assessment as model																		
Assessment greater than model																		
Assessment less than model																		
ELEMENTS FOR ACTION																		

LEVELS OF COMPETENCE

A Appreciation : Know what is meant by the term and what its purpose is.

E Experience : Acquisition of knowledge and skill.

K Knowledge : Understand in some detail the principles of the topic and how they are applied.

B Ability : Application of skill with satisfactory results.

Fold along dotted lines when comparing self-assessment with model competencies

KEY ROLE 9 — HEALTH AND SAFETY

SELF-ASSESSMENT AND AUDIT

	ELEMENTS	HEALTH AND SAFETY LEGISLATION	HEALTH AND SAFETY AT WORK	SAFETY POLICY AND PROCEDURES	SAFETY MANAGEMENT AND EDUCATION													
		1	2	3	4	5	6	7	8	9	10	11	12	13	14	15	16	17
Management level at which Assessment carried out :	B																	
	E																	
	K																	
Date	A																	
Assessment as model																		
Assessment greater than model																		
Assessment less than model																		
ELEMENTS FOR ACTION																		
Management level at which Assessment carried out :	B																	
	E																	
	K																	
Date	A																	
Assessment as model																		
Assessment greater than model																		
Assessment less than model																		
ELEMENTS FOR ACTION																		
Management level at which Assessment carried out :	B																	
	E																	
	K																	
Date	A																	
Assessment as model																		
Assessment greater than model																		
Assessment less than model																		
ELEMENTS FOR ACTION																		

LEVELS OF COMPETENCE

A Appreciation : Know what is meant by the term and what its purpose is.

K Knowledge : Understand in some detail the principles of the topic and how they are applied.

E Experience : Acquisition of knowledge and skill.

B Ability : Application of skill with satisfactory results.

Fold along dotted lines when comparing self-assessment with model competencies

KEY ROLE 10   QUALITY MANAGEMENT

SELF-ASSESSMENT AND AUDIT

	ELEMENTS	QUALITY POLICY AND SYSTEMS	COMPANY MANUALS AND PROCEDURES	QUALITY IMPLEMENTATION															
		1	2	3	4	5	6	7	8	9	10	11	12	13	14	15	16	17
Management level at which	B																	
Assessment carried out :	E																	
	K																	
Date	A																	
Assessment as model																		
Assessment greater than model																		
Assessment less than model																		
ELEMENTS FOR ACTION																		
Management level at which	B																	
Assessment carried out :	E																	
	K																	
Date	A																	
Assessment as model																		
Assessment greater than model																		
Assessment less than model																		
ELEMENTS FOR ACTION																		
Management level at which	B																	
Assessment carried out :	E																	
	K																	
Date	A																	
Assessment as model																		
Assessment greater than model																		
Assessment less than model																		
ELEMENTS FOR ACTION																		

LEVELS OF COMPETENCE

A Appreciation : Know what is meant by the term and what its purpose is.

K Knowledge : Understand in some detail the principles of the topic and how they are applied.

E Experience : Acquisition of knowledge and skill.

B Ability : Application of skill with satisfactory results.

Fold along dotted lines when comparing self-assessment with model competencies